Gold Digger

Jillian Powell

Illustrated by
Alan Down

Badger Publishing

Contents

Chapter 1: Hole in the Ground

The first hole appeared at the end of the garden. It was about the size of a skateboard.

"Must be next door's dog," Mum said. "Digging for bones, or something."

"I don't see how," Dad said. "I mended that gap in the fence, remember?" Then he looked at Jake. "Is this anything to do with you?" he asked.

"No it's not," Jake said. "Why would I want to dig a stupid hole?"

"Perhaps it was a rabbit," piped up Jake's little sister, Sarah.

"It would have to be a rabbit *this* big," Jake scoffed. He held his arms wide apart.

"Well, I can't have holes in my vegetable garden," Mum said. "I put some beans in there a few weeks ago."

"Fill it in, will you Jake?" Dad said. "There's a spade in the shed."

"Why me?" Jake complained. But it was too late. The others had gone indoors. Jake always seemed to get the blame for everything. And the dud jobs like filling in stupid holes.

He took the spade out of the shed and began to fill in the hole. It was very neat, Jake thought. Not like an animal hole. More like a hole that someone had dug carefully. The earth around it was still fresh. It had only just been dug.

A robin sang overhead as Jake worked. Next door's dog began to bark. There was no one else around. But Jake had a strange feeling that he was being watched.

Chapter 2 – Tiddles is Found

The next day was Monday. Jake met his mate Gavin on the way to school.

"Good weekend Jake?"

Jake shrugged. "Went to the match with Dad on Saturday. We lost three nil. Sunday Mum kept nagging me to tidy my room. Oh, and I had to fill in this stupid hole in the vegetable garden."

"Hole?" Gavin said. "You mean hole, like something had been digging?"

"Is there another kind of hole?"

"That's weird," Gavin said. "They had one next door too. Dad said it must be a fox."

"I don't think it was a fox," Jake said. "It was too neat. It didn't look like an animal hole."

"Perhaps there's a vampire on the loose," Gavin said, putting on a scary voice. "Trying to dig itself a grave."

"Oh, yeah. In Mum's vegetable garden," Jake said. He dared not tell Gavin that he felt someone was watching him when he filled in the hole.

The school bell had gone, and for the rest of the day Jake thought no more about holes in the ground - until he was walking home again with Gavin.

"That's your mum, isn't it?" Gavin
said. "With Miss Moore. Looks like the
old dear's upset about something. Miss
Moore, I mean, not your mum," he
added quickly.

Mum had her arm around Miss
Moore. "Come home and have a cup of
tea," she was saying. "It will make you
feel better." Then she spotted Jake.

"Oh, Jake. I'm just taking Miss Moore home for a cuppa," she called. As they went past, Mum nodded towards some bushes in the allotments. Jake and Gavin went over to look. It was getting dark but they could see there was a large hole under one of the bushes.

"Not another one," Gavin said. "You got a torch?"

Jake felt for the flashlight in his school bag. They knelt down and shone it at the hole. As before, the earth was fresh.

"Ugh," Gavin said. "What a stink!"

"Gross!" Jake said, backing away from the smell. Then he held his nose and looked more closely.

This hole was deeper than the others. And it wasn't empty this time. Something was lying at the bottom. Tufts of black fur stuck up here and there through the earth. It was a cat's grave.

"I bet it's Tiddles," Jake said suddenly. "Miss Moore's cat."

Chapter 3 – Buried Treasure

"I thought Tiddles had gone missing," Jake said to Mum later.

"He had. Miss Moore has been looking for him for weeks," Mum told him. "Now she thinks he was run over. Someone buried him under that bush."

"She must be really upset," Jake said.

"Well, she was at first," Mum said. "But at least it means she can stop looking for him. And she thinks it's a sign."

"A sign of what?"

"A sign from Tiddles. That she can have another cat. She was offered a kitten last week, you see. She didn't like to say yes, when she wasn't sure about Tiddles."

Jake told Gavin this on their way to morning Assembly.

"So someone runs over her cat and decides to bury it," Gavin said. "Sort of hit and run."

"Yes, but why did the grave suddenly appear?" Jake asked. "Who dug the cat up?"

Gavin shrugged. Assembly was about to start. Mr Fry, the headmaster, was looking strangely cheerful. After Assembly, he told the school why.

"You will remember the sad event last year when the school sports cups were stolen," he told them. "Well, I have some good news at last. The police had a call yesterday from a man walking his dog near the school playing fields. He has found the cups. The thief had buried them under a tree. The weather, or an animal, had exposed them. So we have our silver cups back!"

Everyone clapped. Jake nudged Gavin in the ribs.

"Don't you see?" he whispered. "Someone had dug them up. It's another hole."

Chapter 4 – Murderer Next Door

There was more to think about when they got home that night. As they turned into Jake's road, they saw a blue light flashing.

"Why is there a police car outside Mr and Mrs Krane's?" Jake said.

"Let's take a look," Gavin said.

The boys went into Jake's garden and looked over the fence. The police had put lines of tape around one area. Inside the tape was a plastic tent with voices coming from it.

"They put a tent up like that when they find a dead body," Gavin said excitedly. "I bet Krane has murdered his wife and buried her in the garden. Have you seen her lately?"

Jake shook his head.

"There you go then," Gavin said. "Exposing Tiddles' grave was probably a warning to Krane. Someone knows what he did. The police had a tip-off. Now they are digging her up."

"Shut up, that's awful," Jake hissed.

"Well, why else would they have the tent up?" Gavin said. "They do that so you can't see…"

"Okay, okay. No need to go into detail," Jake said.

This was getting stranger and stranger. First Tiddles, then the school cups, and now… Surely Krane wasn't a murderer? But Gavin was right - the tent, the tape, several police officers - it did look serious.

"What if it wasn't a tip off?" he said to Gavin. "What if the grave had sort of opened up… on its own?"

"Don't get you," Gavin said.

"Well, don't you think it's a bit odd - all these holes opening up? And they're not just holes, are they? Someone is uncovering things."

"Yeah, but who wants to uncover a dead cat? Or the school cups, for that matter?" Gavin said. "I mean, what's in it for them?"

"I don't know," Jake said thoughtfully. "Maybe they're looking for something." He looked over at the vegetable garden. The earth was still dark around the hole he had filled in. What if something was buried there?

"Tell you what," Gavin said. "It's night when it happens, right? This mystery digging. So we'll keep watch. And if someone is out there, we'll catch him."

Chapter 5 – A Dark Alley

Jake crept out of his room just after midnight. He had agreed to meet Gavin in the alley beside Krane's house. There was no moon so he flashed his torch along the alley. No sign of Gavin.

An owl hooted. Jake began to feel cold and a bit scared. Step by step, he crept along the alley. Then he heard it. The sound of a spade sliding into the ground. The clink of a stone as the earth was dug out. Someone was out there. Digging at midnight.

Where on earth was Gavin? Jake looked this way and that, up and down the alley. Then he turned to ice.

A figure was blocking the alley. It
was dressed in black and carried a dim
lantern. It came nearer. Jake could just
make out a bony white face. He
opened his mouth to speak but nothing
came out.

Then the creature lifted the lantern
to its face. Slowly, the white bones
peeled away. It was Gavin, wearing
last year's Halloween mask.

"Idiot!" Jake said. "You scared me to death."

Gavin laughed. "That got you going! I am the mystery digger," he said in a deep, ghostly voice.

"So it was you... just now... digging?" Jake said, relieved.

"Nothing to do with me," said Gavin, puzzled. "It took ages finding this stupid mask."

"But I heard it," Jake insisted. "It was coming from the gardens..."

"Probably Krane's," Gavin said. "Maybe he's moving the body."

They crept down the alley into Krane's garden. The tent was shut up for the night. Police tape stopped them going further.

Suddenly, a light shone in their faces and Krane appeared at a window.

"What's going on?"

"We… We heard… that is…"

"Heard about it and wanted to take a look did you?" Krane said, calmly. "Well, I suppose it's only natural."

"Have the police gone?" Gavin asked. He was wondering why Krane hadn't been arrested.

21

"The police have gone. The experts will be back tomorrow," Krane told them matter-of-factly.

"So she's still in there?" Jake muttered.

"Oh, yes. She's still there. Been there for years."

"Then… how did they find her?" Gavin asked.

"Well, that's the strange thing," Krane told them. "A dog or something had been digging. A bit of her was sticking up out of the ground."

Jake and Gavin looked horrified. Which bit, Jake wondered. A hand? A leg?

"It was lucky really," Krane went on. "I was planning to put a fish pond there. Might have blown myself up."

The boys looked blank.

"She's a big bomb, you know," Krane said. "Must have come down in the Blitz. Been lying there all these years in my garden, and I had no idea. I can't let you see tonight. Too dangerous. But perhaps when the experts have done their bit…"

So that explained the tent and the tape, Jake thought. But it still didn't explain who, or what, kept digging holes in the middle of the night, uncovering secrets as they went.

Chapter 6 – Jake's Discovery

On Saturday, Jake had an idea. Dad had been called into work and Mum and Sarah had gone shopping, so Jake went down to the garden shed, took a spade and began digging in the vegetable garden. Beans were pushing up through the earth, except for the patch where the hole had been. Jake worked quickly, throwing aside the earth.

Then he knelt down and looked in the hole. Earth and stones. A bit of old china. What was that? Jake peered closer. Something glinted in the sunlight. He scratched at the earth. There was a brilliant flash of light.

It was a ring! Jake picked it up and rubbed it on his sleeve. It was Mum's diamond engagement ring! She had been really upset when she lost it a few weeks ago. It must have come off when she was planting the beans. Jake put the ring carefully in his pocket.

Now Jake felt sure that whatever had dug the hole had been looking for something else. "Something that will help someone," he thought. "And it won't stop till it finds it." As he filled in the hole, Jake had the same feeling as before. He was being watched.

When Jake went indoors, Mum and Dad were in the kitchen. Sarah was crying.

"Guess what, Mum? I've found your ring."

"Oh, Jake. That's marvellous," Mum said, hugging him. She slipped the ring back on her finger. "We could do with something nice happening."

Jake looked at Dad. He looked really worried.

"I've had some bad news, Jake. The firm are closing up. I'm out of a job."

"Dad says we may have to move," Sarah said miserably. "I don't want to leave this house."

"None of us does, dear," Mum said. "But we might have to."

Jake was silent. Suddenly, the mystery holes didn't seem important any more.

Chapter 7 – Night Journey

Jake couldn't sleep. He lay there, tossing and turning. A bright moon was shining across his bed. He got up to close the curtains. Was anyone out there digging tonight? Jake opened the window and listened. The gardens were all quiet. But there was a strange rumbling sound.

There it was again. It sounded as if a huge machine was rumbling backwards and forwards. A digger. Could anyone be working at night?

It was no use trying to sleep. Jake quickly put on his clothes and trainers and crept downstairs. The others were all sleeping. Jake let himself out of the front door and followed the sound.

At the end of the road was a tall
fence. They were going to build new
houses on the land behind. They hadn't
started work yet... but that's where the
sound was coming from. Jake crept
through a gap in the fence. The
rumbling became a roar.

Headlights shone in his eyes. Jake backed up against the fence as a vast yellow monster thundered towards him. Its giant wheels were taller than he was. A jagged claw, like a dinosaur's jaws, was heading right at him. Nothing stopped it - it tossed stones, earth, everything out of its way. It came closer and closer, as if it was going to hurl him out of its way too - like a rag doll.

"Stop, stop!" Jake shouted at the cab. Then he froze. There was no driver. The cab was empty. But the machine kept coming. Its great yellow claw swung ever closer. Jake's heart banged against his ribs.

.

He spun round, smashing at the fence, forcing his way back through the gap. Then he ran and ran. He didn't stop until he reached his own front door.

Chapter 8 – Treasure Trove

In the morning, Jake looked at the chalky earth on his trainers. There had to be some explanation. He got out of bed and went over to the computer.

Later, he was waiting for Gavin outside the school gates. He wanted to tell him about his night-time encounter with the digger. And he had something to show him.

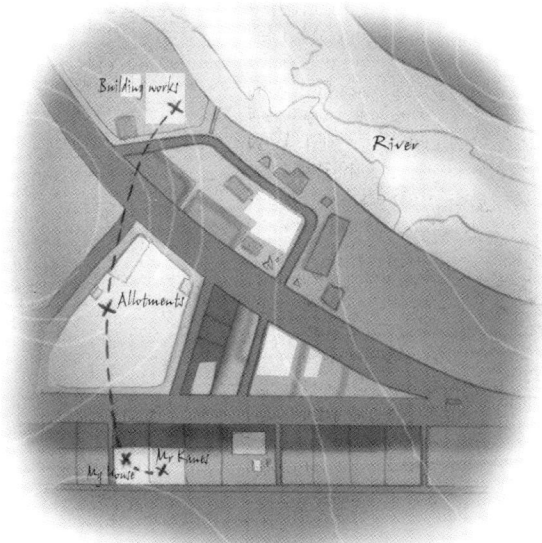

"I did it on the computer," he told Gavin. "I've marked all the holes - every one of them. And look, they're in a line, getting closer and closer to this patch of land. Whatever our mystery digger is looking for, it's in there."

"But they're about to build on that land," Gavin reminded him.

"Exactly!" Jake said. "The digger has to find whatever it's looking for, before it's too late."

"But why did it dig up Tiddles and the school cups?" Gavin looked puzzled.

"I don't know," Jake said. "But my granddad's always going on about energy lines under the earth. Maybe stuff that's buried gives off some sort of energy."

"Wicked! And this digger is some sort of ghostly metal detector?" Gavin said.

"Will you come back there with me?" he asked Gavin. "I don't want to face that thing again on my own."

Gavin pulled a face. "What do you want me to do, feed it stones?"

But he was waiting for Jake after school. Together, they found the gap in the fence and climbed in. They looked round.

There was no digger.

Even more strange, there was no way in or out of the site, except for the small gap in the fence.

"No machine could get in here,"
Gavin said. "You must have imagined
it."

"So how d'you explain these giant
holes?" asked Jake. Enormous holes
had been dug all over the site. It was
like being on the moon.

One hole was much bigger than the
rest. Jake climbed down into it.

"Any dead cats down there?" Gavin joked.

"Lend me your penknife," Jake called back.

He began scratching at the chalk with the knife. If he was right, he would find something that had been long buried; something that would help someone - just like in all the other holes.

After a few minutes, Gavin began to get impatient. "Come on, Jake. There's nothing down there."

"Wait!" snapped Jake. And he set to work on another part of the hole. A moment later, he let out a yell. "YES!"

Jake had uncovered a metal corner.

He scraped away at the chalk around it. Little by little, a metal box appeared. Gently, he pulled it free. Gavin was in the hole with him by now. "Open it, Jake," he said.

The lid was stiff. In the end, Jake had to use the pen knife to open it. As they lifted the lid, Gavin gasped. "Wow! Rings, coins, necklaces..."

"We've found a treasure trove, I'm sure of it," said Jake. "I bet this was what the digger was looking for."

****

Three months later, Jake and Gavin went to see their treasure trove in the local museum. The experts said it was one of the most important finds in the area. Their share of money as finders helped Jake's family stay in their house while Dad found a new job.

Gavin never believed Jake's story about the ghost digger. And Jake never told anyone else what he had seen that night. He knew now that the digger was trying to help him, not hurt him.

And no more holes were dug. Except for one.

At the bottom of the garden, behind the shed, Jake dug a hole. The museum had let him keep one small ring from the hoard. Carefully, he laid it in the hole.

"One day, I hope someone will find this," he said aloud. "Someone who needs it, like my family needed the treasure trove."

Then he filled in the hole. No one would know that the ring was there... except Jake, and the ghost digger.

Other Badger Reading Titles

Stories with familiar settings
Sam and Shrimp   Chris Buckton
Here Comes Trouble!   Chris Buckton
Shop Till You Drop   Chris Buckton

Adventure and Mystery stories
Mysterious?   David Orme
Stranded in the Desert   Jillian Powell
Ghost Digger   Jillian Powell

Historical stories
Home Front   Chris Buckton
A Shield of Honour   Jonny Zucker
Through Twisting Streets   Jonny Zucker

Stories that raise issues
Getting Even   Jonny Zucker
Thief in the Camp   Jillian Powell
Jenny's Story   David Orme

Badger Publishing Limited
26 Wedgwood Way, Pin Green Industrial Estate,
Stevenage, Hertfordshire SG1 4QF
Telephone: 01438 356907   Fax: 01438 747015
www.badger-publishing.co.uk   enquiries@badger-publishing.co.uk

Ghost Digger ISBN 1 84424 092 4

Text © Jillian Powell 2003   Series editing © Leonie Bennett
Complete work © Badger Publishing Limited 2003

Series Editor: Leonie Bennett   Editor: Paul Martin
Publisher: David Jamieson   Cover design: Cathy May
Illustrations: Alan Down (Beehive Illustration Agency)